How To Make

Step By Step Guide on How to Make Your Very Own Bangles at Home

(With 30 Projects to Get You Started)

How to Make Bangles

Introduction

Do you love wearing bangles and want to have as many as possible, but that seems challenging because good jewelry can be quite expensive?

Do you have some time on your hands and would not mind learning to make some amazing statement bangles?

Well, you are in luck as you have stumbled upon a simple guidebook to making bangle. This book will teach you the basics of creating simple or intricate bangles. You will learn all you need to know: from the materials used to the different bangle styles and designs, tools, supplies, and so much more.

The book also has 30 super easy projects of different types of bangles to get you started. Brace yourself for a fun and exciting journey of learning to make bangles at home and improve your sense of fashion.

Table of Contents

Introduction 2

Chapter 1: The Basics 7

Bangle Designs 7

Bangle Structures 8

Material Used To Make Bangles 9

Other Materials Used For Making Bangles 10

The Bangle Style 12

Common Tools And Supplies Used For Making Bangles 15

Chapter 2: Clay Bangles 17

Polymer Clay Bangles 17

Floral Stamped Clay Bangles 19

DIY Clay Bangles 22

Easy Polymer Clay Bangle 24

DIY Braided Clay Bangle 27

Chapter 3: Plastic Bangles 29

Bangle From A Plastic Bottle 29

DIY Plastic Bangle Bracelets 33

Plastic Bangles With Fabric 35

Bangle From Recycled Plastic 37

DIY Vinyl Tube Bangle 40

Chapter 4: Metal Bangles............................ 43

Simple Stamped Charm Bangle 43

Simple Hammered Silver Bangles 46

Pierce Metal Leaf Charm Bangle.......................... 52

Metal Stamped Bangle Cuffs................................ 56

Boho Chic Rainbow Bangle Bracelets 59

Chapter 5: Simple Woven Bangle Projects . 62

Woven Bangle 62

Woven Yarn Bangles 66

Easy Woven Bangle Bracelet 71

Fun Accessory DIY Yarn Woven Bangles 74

Chapter 6: Simple Wooden Bangle Projects 78

Wire Wrapped Wooden Bangle 78

Painted Wooden Bangles 81

Wooden Bangles For Animal Lovers 85

DIY Mod Podge Wood Bangle Bracelets 87

Chapter 7: Simple Fabric Bangle Projects ..89

No-Sew Simple Fabric Bangle Bracelet 89

Quick And Easy DIY Fabric Bangle 92

DIY Bangle From Fabric And Hanger 95

Upcycle Scrap Fabric into Wrapped Bangles 97

Chapter 7: Other Simple Bangle Projects . 100

DIY Criss Cross Leather And Chain Bangle 100

DIY Dainty Washer Bracelet 106

Harlequin Decoupage Bangle 111

Coral And Sea Shell Resin Bangles 115

DIY Zipper Bangle Bracelets 118

How To Make Thread Bangles 121

Easy-to-Make Delicate Beaded Bangles 124

Chapter 8: Where To Begin 129

Helpful Tips On How To Style Your Bangles 133

Conclusion 137

Chapter 1: The Basics

Let's discuss some basic things about bangles and the art of making them:

Bangle Designs

Unlike bracelets, bangles take on more of a circular shape and are rigid. In the past, they made bangles from terracotta and glass and embellishments from copper, shells, glass, stones, and other similar materials.

Nowadays, you can find bangles made from various materials, from simple plain designs to embellished and intricately shaped jewelry pieces that incorporate gemstones and precious metals.

We can classify bangles according to:

- Style
- The material we make them from
- Their structure

Sure, the material and structure of the bangle are essential. However, their style is what makes them unique.

How to Make Bangles

Bangle Structures

Solid cylinder bangles: This is a round-shaped continuous loop cylinder that you simply slide over your wrist. It is perhaps the most recognizable and popular type as it's the initial design worn by women from South Asian cultures.

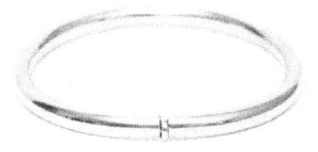

Split cylindrical bangles: As suggested by the name, these bangles split from the center and include a closing and opening feature. This gives split cylindrical bangles a more snug fit than solid cylindrical ones.

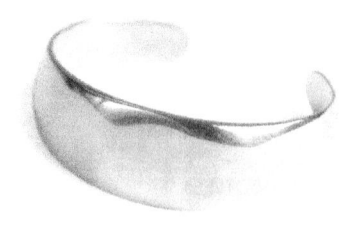

Cuff bangles: These bangles take on a sturdier and chunkier appearance. Cuff bangles are the most recent bangle structure of the rest.

Material Used To Make Bangles

Many different materials can make bangles, from wood to glass, but the most common is metal. Below are the most commonly used metals:

Silver: Silver is suitable for making bangles as it is soft, ductile, and malleable. It also has durable, reflective qualities, and you can polish it to a luminous sheen.

Gold: In its pure form, gold is bright reddish-yellow and doesn't tarnish. Like silver, gold is a precious metal of antiquity and is among the most ductile and malleable metals. Gold is alloyed with palladium, nickel, zinc, silver, or copper when making jewelry such as bangles to yield a harder material. You can produce green, rose, white, and yellow gold during the alloying process, giving you various choices. Gold is also one of the most durable metals and is less allergenic than silver.

Platinum: This precious metal is silver-white and is among the rarest resources in the entire globe, which explains its correspondence to luxury as in platinum credit cards and platinum records. Compared to gold, platinum is highly dense and less malleable. It is also four times stronger and approximately 30 times rarer than gold.

Due to the hardness of this material, it is usually mixed with other metals like titanium, iridium, rhodium, palladium, and copper to make it more malleable. Platinum also never tarnishes and is durable and hypoallergenic, making it suitable for people with sensitive skin.

Titanium: This high-strength metal is lustrous and has a silver color. It is lightweight, scratch-resistant, corrosion-resistant, easy to color, and completely hypoallergenic. Titanium is usually mixed with other metals to make it more malleable.

Other Materials Used For Making Bangles

Wood: Hardwoods are the most preferred for making bangles and any other jewelry, but you can use any wood; however, the finish, color, and grain of the wood may have a hand in the one you select for your design. Wood is easy to cut, carve, shape, and polish to make chunky lightweight bangles.

Using storm-felled, recycled, or salvaged wood in making jewelry has been re-popularized by the need to use eco-friendly materials. However, you must be careful with your wooden bangles as they are prone to bashes, bumps, and knocks.

Glass: We can use various glass forms to design bangles like sea glass, lampwork, fused glass (dichroic and art glass), and Murano (Millefiori and Venetian). You can heat glass and fuse it into bangles or use it in its natural form, like beach glass (sea glass). Cold glass can also be ground, drilled, cut, polished, and engraved to meet your aesthetic desire. glass comes in many colors and can be used to create many shapes. However, this material is very fragile and easy to chip or break.

Plastic: Plastic is lightweight with strong plasticity. Bangles made from this material are usually very cheap and not that durable. The good thing about plastic is that it's ductile and easily malleable.

Ceramic: In making jewelry such as bangles, this material incorporates precious metal alloy powder and high-precision ceramics. The two components are mixed and fired together,

How to Make Bangles

then made into a bangle after a couple of processes and continuous polishing and grinding. The color of the jewelry piece depends on the ingredients of the precious metal alloy powder.

Bangles made from ceramic are comfortable to wear, resistant, light, and anti-sensitive.

Gemstones (and stones): Some of the most popular gemstones used for making bangles are sapphire, emerald, ruby, and diamond. The type of gemstone or stone you pick can depend on how it feels (the energy or texture it gives you), how it looks (the shape, color, grain), a special memory it gives you, and what the stone means to you, where you got it from (recycled, found on a beach, or a stone local to your area).

Stones and gemstones come in various colors, textures, and finishes. These materials can be cut, carved, polished, faceted, drilled, and manipulated in various ways. However, working with stones and gemstones is expensive as they require special diamond tools.

The Bangle Style

Then we also have the style. This breathes life into bangles and keeps this piece of jewelry in demand. Each bangle has its style that makes it relevant and unique. The different bangle styles include:

- **Interlocked bangles:** In this style, the bangles are interlaced as a stack of three (or more) like trinity rings, giving the piece of jewelry a boho look. You can spice things further by mixing three different colors and three distinct metals.

- **Bangles embellished with gemstones:** These bangles were pioneered during the Art Deco period in Europe and have continued to spread ever since. We can arrange the gemstones in several ways.

How to Make Bangles

- **Plain bangles:** This style has remained timeless through the centuries. Plain bangles can be subtle but unique enough to complement your look without much effort. Whether made of glass or metal, plain bangles rank highly in the jewelry world. A set of these bangles makes an ideal choice for multiple outfits and different occasions.

Common Tools And Supplies Used For Making Bangles

- **Ruler:** This basic tool is something you probably have already. I recommend you get a graphing ruler as it is transparent and can help you visualize better.

- **Round-nose pliers:** This tool helps form loops, bends, jump rings, and clasps. You can also use them with other pliers to pry open chains, rings, and loops.

- **Chain-nose pliers:** We use this tool to pry things open for bending and crimping.

- **Wire cutters:** This tool cuts rings, cords, chains, wires, and more.

- **Practice material:** Until you can be sure you know what you are doing, you will need practice material. You can get acquainted with this art using copper or another base metal wire instead of wasting your resources on valuable metals.

- **Disk punch:** If you want to cut repeated even shapes of squares, circles, or hearts, this is the tool for you. A disk punch will help you produce identical shapes consistently.

How to Make Bangles

Now that you know the different materials you can use to make bangles and the various bangle structures and styles, you have all the basics you need to start making bangles.

Below are simple projects you can try out to get started with making bangles:

Chapter 2: Clay Bangles

Here are some clay bangles projects for your practice purposes:

Polymer Clay Bangles

Supplies

Empty metal cans – for the bangle form

Sculpey clay color set

Directions

Step 1: Choose the color palette you want to use. This project used the rainbow color set.

Step 2: Soften up each color individually by kneading with your hands.

Step 3: Roll either color out to form a long strand, then lay them together to create stripes.

How to Make Bangles

Step 4: Use a rolling pin to flatten your strands of clay. Since the continuous loop bangle is less fragile as it does not undergo bending, ensure to make it thinner than the open cuff style. For this project, it was around 1/8 inch thick.

Step 5: Grab your can and wrap the strands of clay around it, then trim for an even seam. Bond the clay by pressing the seam edges together.

Step 6: Bake the clay according to the instructions of the manufacturer. For the Sculpey clay used in this project, the recommendations were to bake every ¼ inch of thickness at 275 degrees F for 15 minutes.

Step 7: Once the timer on the oven goes off, remove the baked bangles and leave them to cool.

Step 8: Grab your butter knife and gently slide it in between the can and the inner side of the clay to release the bangle.

Floral Stamped Clay Bangles

Supplies

Cookie cutters of 3-4 inch diameter

An embossed glass plate or any other item with a deep relief embossment

Oven-baked polymer clay in your preferred colors

Clay glazes or nail polish for finishing – select a color that closely matches the clay but is a bit brighter.

7/8 inch ribbon

*You can leave the clay as it is without glazing if desired.

How to Make Bangles

Directions

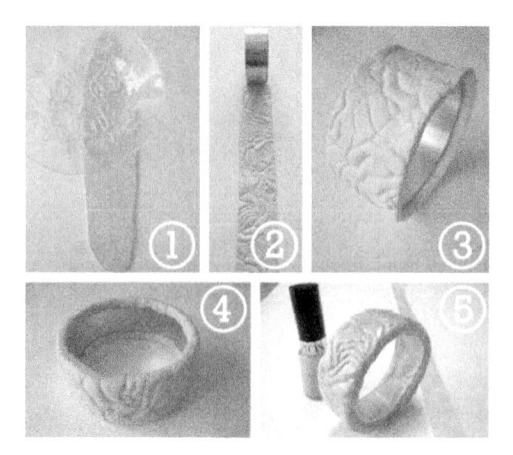

Step 1: Knead the clay to soften it, then roll it out to a thickness of about 1/8 inches. Ensure that the strip length is enough for the entire perimeter of your cookie cutter.

Step 2: Stamp the pattern onto the strip of clay.

Step 3: Cut the clay using a pizza cutter or knife, leaving an additional ¼ inch on either side of the cookie cutter.

Step 4: Roll the clay onto your cookie-cutter, then gently trim and connect the seams.

Step 5: Fold the edges of the clay and flatten them to the inside of the cookie cutter. Place your design in the oven and bake according to the manufacturer's directions.

Step 6: Allow the bangles to cool before glazing with nail polish. Leave to dry.

Step 7: Attach the ribbon to the inner side of the cookie-cutter using heavy-duty double-sided tape or glue.

How to Make Bangles

DIY Clay Bangles

Supplies

Sculpey clay or any other heat-setting clay– in a variety of your preferred colors

Directions

Step 1: Roll out a chunk of clay in your hands.

Step 2: You can try making a braided three-strand pattern, maybe a twisted two-strand pattern or a mixture of colors rolled out together.

Step 3: Roll out your clay to a length of approximately 8 inches.

Step 4: Press the ends together to create a tight seal.

Step 5: Preheat your oven to 275 degrees F

Step 6: Transfer the bangle to a baking sheet and bake it for around 15 minutes. Let it cool.

Optional: You can glaze the bangles to give them a glossy finish.

How to Make Bangles

Easy Polymer Clay Bangle

Supplies

Polymer clay

Egg ring

Directions

Step 1: Knead the clay in your hands to smooth it, then form it into a thin sheet

Step 2: Press the sheet of clay on the inner side of the egg ring.

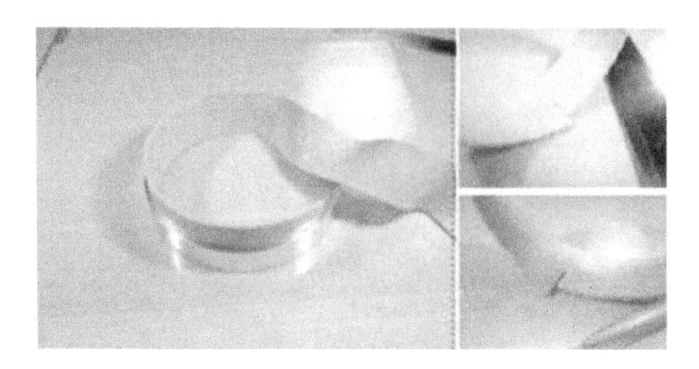

Step 3: Once the clay overlaps, trim off the excess, then use a smoothing tool to smooth out the seam.

Step 4: Trim off the excess from both edges, then texture the clay with coarse sandpaper —if desired.

Step 5: Form another sheet of clay about 2-3mm wider than your egg ring on both edges and position the egg ring over it.

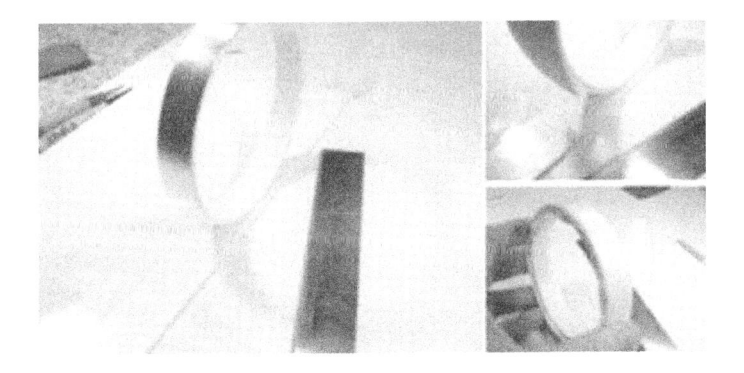

Step 6: Once the clay overlaps, trim the excess off, then smoothen the seam.

Step 7: Fold the clay over the bangle gently, then press it to the inner clay inside the ring. The entire ring should be covered in clay.

How to Make Bangles

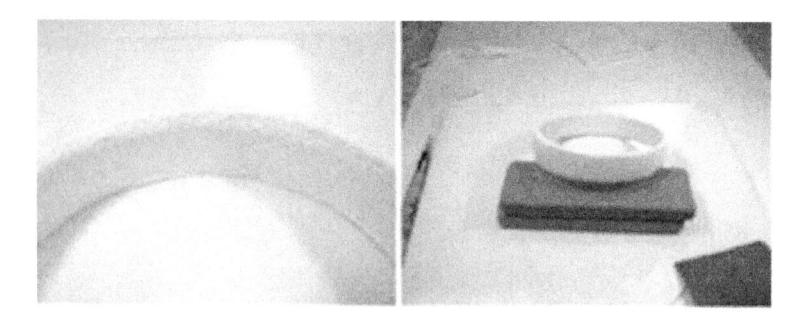

Step 8: Smooth out each seam and retexture.

Step 9: Decorate your bangle as desired.

DIY Braided Clay Bangle

Supplies

Razor blade

Clay

Directions

Step 1: Soften the clay up by kneading it with your hands

Step 2: Roll out three long tubes using the palm of your hands

Step 3: Press together the top of the clay strips and start braiding as shown below:

How to Make Bangles

Step 4: Use your wrist to determine the length of your bangle, then slice off the excess using a razor blade.

Step 5: Press together both ends, then place in the oven and bake at 245 degrees F for 25 minutes.

Chapter 3: Plastic Bangles

Here are some bangle-making projects involving plastic:

Bangle From A Plastic Bottle

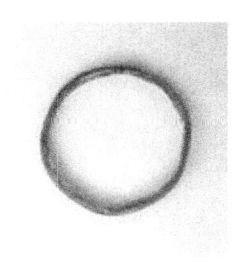

Supplies

Iron

Scissors

Knife

Plastic bottle

Directions

Step 1: If your plastic bottle has a sticker, start by stripping it off.

Step 2: Use the knife to cut the bottle in half.

How to Make Bangles

Step 3: Cut out multiple rings from your bottle, each with a thickness of approximately 0.6 to 0.7 inches. (Cut along the straight ridges if your bottle has them.)

Step 4: Use a pair of scissors to trim the edges. If necessary, wash and dry the rings well.

Step 5: Allow the iron to heat to its highest temperature. Press the edges of your plastic ring to the iron for a couple of seconds. Doing this will result in the edges of your ring curling inwards—repeat around all edges of each ring.

Step 6: If your bangle doesn't appear round enough, press it to the iron, then correct its shape while the plastic is still warm and hold it in place until it is completely cool.

Step 7: Confirm whether the inner diameter of the bangles fits. As you apply heat to the rings, the diameter decreases by approximately 0.3-0.4 inches.

Step 8: If the bangle is still too big for you, you can try reducing the diameter by cutting the bangle in one place, then sliding one end into the other end.

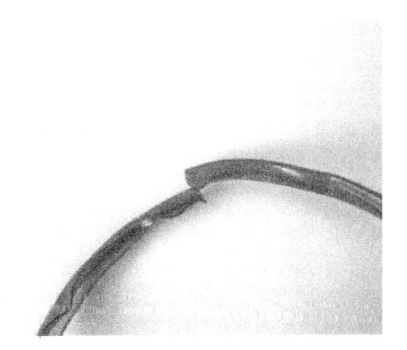

Step 9: Press where the two edges overlap on the hot iron to have the edges of the inner end and the outer one fit each other well, as shown below:

How to Make Bangles

You may adjust the diameter of each bangle or only the one you'll be wearing last.

DIY Plastic Bangle Bracelets

Supplies

Nail polish or permanent markers (You may also use food coloring and school glue)

Iron

Utility knife

Scissors

Clear plastic bottles with stickers and glue removed (we used 1-liter bottles where each yields three bangles)

Directions

Step 1: To begin, make a small slit where the plastic bottle widens.

How to Make Bangles

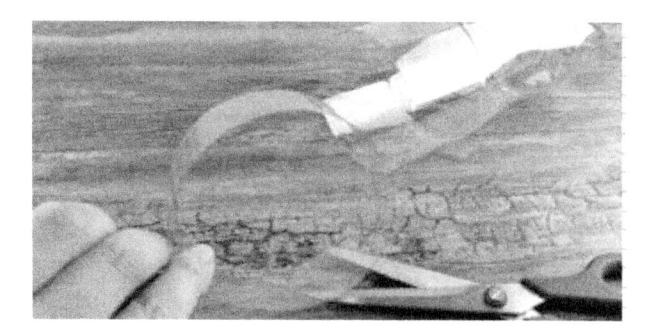

Step 2: Grab a pair of scissors and cut across the bottle.

Step 3: Repeat the same about 1 inch down, and you'll have one ring.

Step 4: Heat your iron to the maximum temperature

Step 5: Carefully press both edges of your ring on the hot iron for a couple of seconds until the edge forms a curl.

Step 6: All that's left is to decorate the inner side of the bangle. Add designs and color to your piece of jewelry using glue paint, nail polish, or markers. Let it dry completely.

Plastic Bangles With Fabric

Supplies

Scissors

A piece of fabric

Plastic bottle

Glue

Directions

Step 1: Cut along the straight ridges of your plastic bottle to form a ring. The rings in this project were around 3-5 cm.

Step 2: Use your scissors to cut a strip of fabric a little wider than the plastic ring.

Step 3: Apply glue to your bangle's inner and outer sides.

How to Make Bangles

Step 4: Wrap the piece of fabric around the plastic ring so that the edges overlap on the inner side of the bangle. Secure the edges with more glue.

Bangle From Recycled Plastic

Supplies

Blow pen

Art knife

Ruler

Scissors

Pen

Plastic soda bottle

Iron

Clear acrylic sealer spray

Directions

How to Make Bangles

Step 1: Determine the width you want for your bangle. For this project, it was 4.5 cm.

Step 2: Cut across the bottle to create a ring of your desired width.

Step 3: Use Blo pens to paint on your bangle, then seal the paint using Acrylic crystal clear spray.

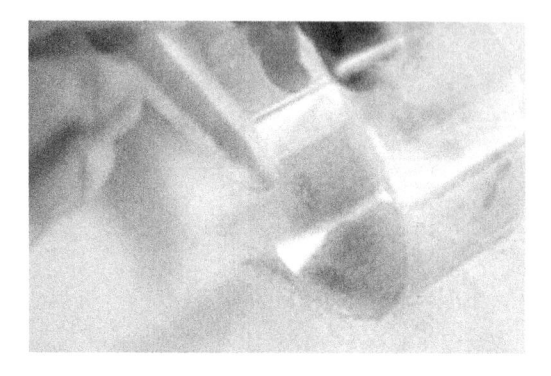

Step 4: Heat your iron to medium heat.

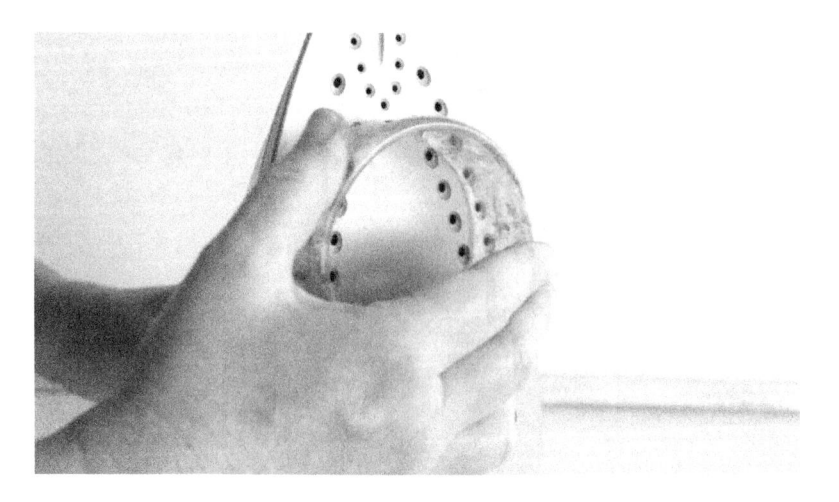

Step 5: Touch the plastic ring to the iron, moving it in a circular motion until either end starts curling inwards.

How to Make Bangles

DIY Vinyl Tube Bangle

Supplies

3/8 inch PVC vinyl tubing

¼ inch clear PVC vinyl tubing

Duct tape or painter's tape – this project used Frog Tape

Scissors

Glitter (chunky, fine, shaped, a blend of everything), rhinestones or beads

A tiny funnel for the glitter – you can also try making a small cone using tape and a piece of paper.

A strip of fabric or ribbon for covering the "connecting" tube —this project used some bias tape.

Directions

Step 1: Cut out a strip of the ¼-inch vinyl tubing to be a little shorter than the measurement of your wrist length.

Step 2: Cut out 0.5 inches of the 3/8 vinyl tubing for connecting the ends once you complete your design.

Step 3: Grab the strip of the ¼-inch vinyl tubing and seal off one end using tape to prevent the glitter from spilling out.

Step 4: Insert the small funnel into the other open end and hold it still with your hand.

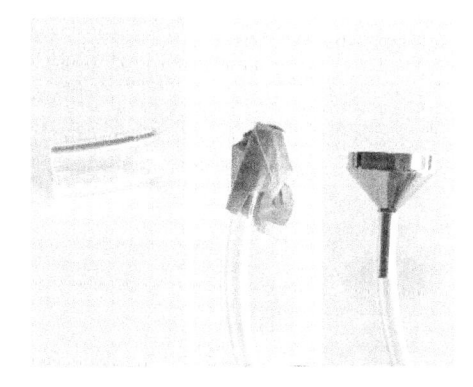

Step 5: Pour the glitter in carefully through the funnel. Add as much glitter as you like. For this project, I filled the glitter in the tubing so that it couldn't move freely.

How to Make Bangles

You can help the glitter move down the tube by tapping it; just don't shake the funnel.

Step 6: After filling the glitter, insert the 3/8 inch tubing piece into the open end of your bangle. Do this slowly and carefully to avoid spilling the glitter everywhere.

Step 7: Holding your thumb over the open connector tubing, carefully remove the tape sealing the other end. Now join this end to the connector tubing to complete the bangle.

Optional: Tie off the joining section with a bow.

Chapter 4: Metal Bangles

Simple Stamped Charm Bangle

Supplies

Eyelet setting tool

Bracelet bending pliers

Stamping supplies

3.7mm eyelets – this project used a silver finish

Small 2-hole punch for a 3/32" hole

Hammer and Steel Bench block

Jump rings, jewelry pliers, and a charm

How to Make Bangles

¼ inch aluminum bracelet blank

Directions

Step 1: Begin by stamping your blank with a phrase or message of your choice and punch a 3/32" hole. For this project, I situated the hole slightly lower than the middle so that the charm would look like it was at the bottom of the bangle though it doesn't really matter where you put it so long as you don't punch beyond the edge of your blank.

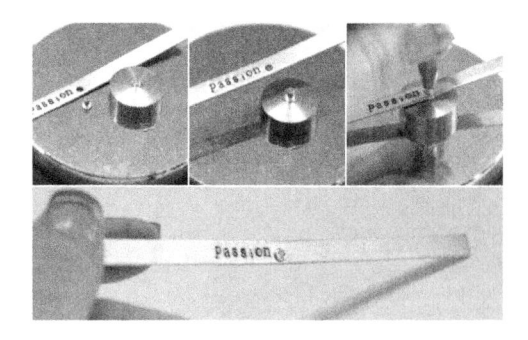

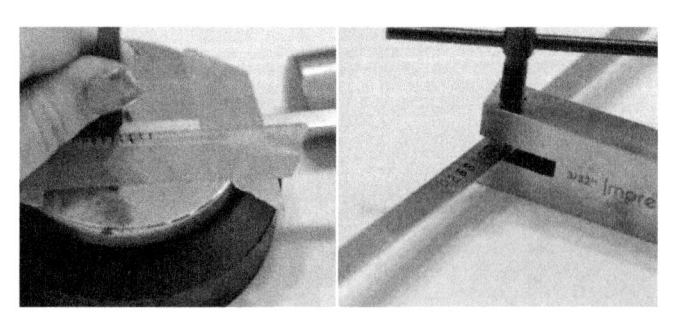

Step 2: What follows is setting the eyelet. Position the base of your eyelet setter over the steel bench block. (When you place it on a soft surface such as a wooden table, it will probably

damage the surface.) Place the eyelet on the base ring, then position the blank over the eyelet. Set your setter tool to fit into the grooves of the eyelet when it comes up through the hole you pierce on the blank.

Step 3: Hammer the setter tool from the top until it flattens onto the blank - it took about 6 to 8 taps for this project. Whether you set the eyelet from the back or front of the blank, you'll get a smoothly finished hole.

Step 4: The next thing is bending the blank into a wearable curve. You simply go around the bangle with bending pliers to form a continuous curve.

Step 5: Attach the charm to your piece using a jump ring. You may also want to smooth the sharp edges of your bangle using a small file so that it doesn't scratch you when you wear it.

How to Make Bangles

Simple Hammered Silver Bangles

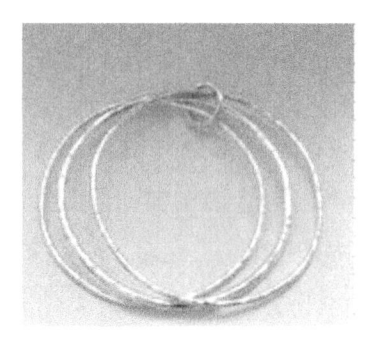

Supplies

4cm Fully annealed 3.00mm sterling silver round wire

0.50mm x 3.0mm x 600mm Easy silver solder strip

152 mm ruler

0.70mm x 1.5mm x 600mm Medium silver soldier strip

76mm adjustable saw frame

2mm sterling silver round wire

Standard brass tweezers

Camel hair flux brush

130mm Half round pliers, plain pliers

Hand torch

3 lb barrel tumbling machine with metal polishing kit

Large round jump ring maker

32mm Repousse hammer

50mm – 75mm Durston cast iron round bracelet mandrel with tang

Vintaj Steel block

Ceramic dish soldering set and borax dried flux bar

150g Picklean safe pickling powder

Directions

Step 1: To make a pure silver bangle with a diameter of around 7cm, measure and cut out 22cm strips from the silver wire. Use a piercing saw to cut the silver wire, then file the ends using a needle file. You can then use a fine-grade emery paper for further smoothening.

Step 2: Bring the ends of the bangle together using half-round pliers. At this point, you don't have to worry about having a perfect circle, though it is best to ensure the connection is good and tight. If necessary, file the bangle using a flat-sided needle file.

How to Make Bangles

Step 3: Thoroughly flux the joint where the two ends meet, then apply some of the medium solder strips. Heat the whole bangle before soldering the ends of your silver bangle.

Step 4: Pickle the bangle, then use emery paper to clean the joint.

Step 5: Position the bangle around the mandrel, then use your Repousse hammer to hammer all the way around. To make your work easier and neat, hold the hammer at a fixed angle and ensure you rotate the bangle.

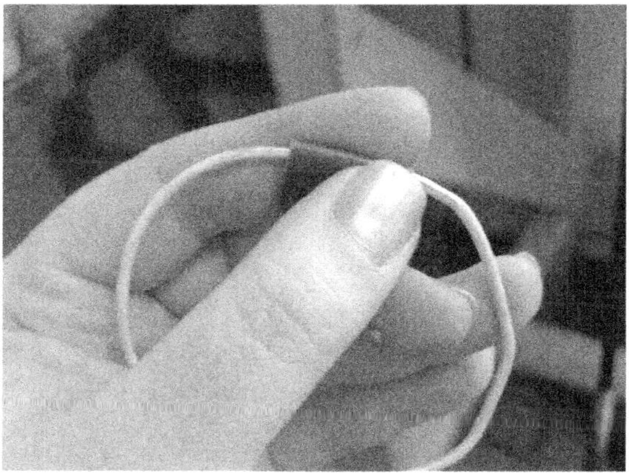

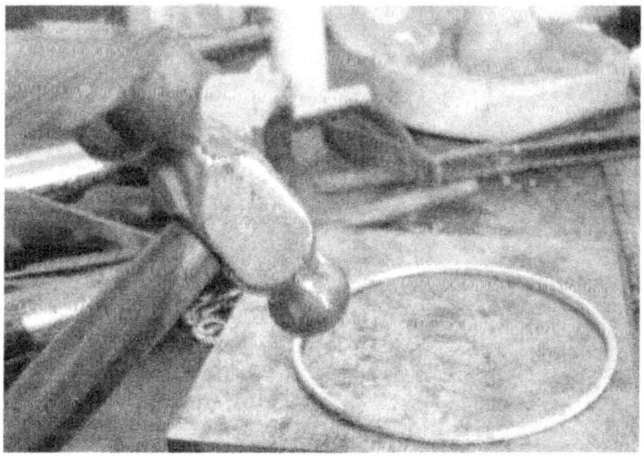

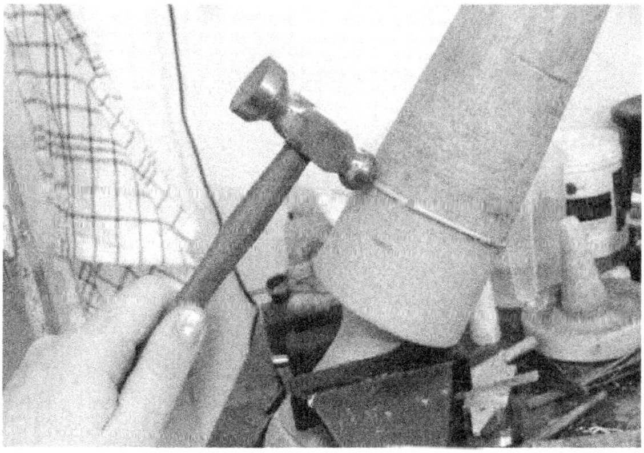

How to Make Bangles

Position your bangle on an anvil or steel block and hammer all across. Flip over the bangle and hammer the same way on the other side.

Redo steps 1-5 using the 3mm and 2mm wires to have all three silver bangles.

Step 6: Repeat steps 1-4 using the fully annealed 3mm round wire. Solder the ring the same way but using the easy solder. Place the small ring around a jump ring or ring mandrel, then hammer the sides of the ring.

Step 7: Cut through the solder join once the ring is perfectly round. This is the best way to ensure the binding ring turns out perfectly circular.

Step 8: Hold your binding ring up using soldering pliers and open it up, then insert the 3 hammered silver bangles inside it. Flux the ends of the rings, then apply the easy solder. You may also use a solder paste in place of the easy solder. If using the paste, you won't need flux as it's included in the mixture. Solder the join.

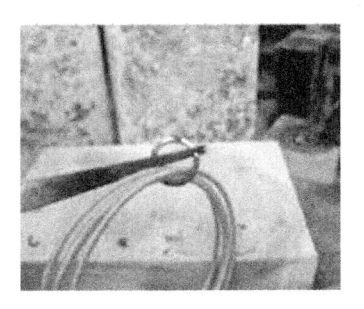

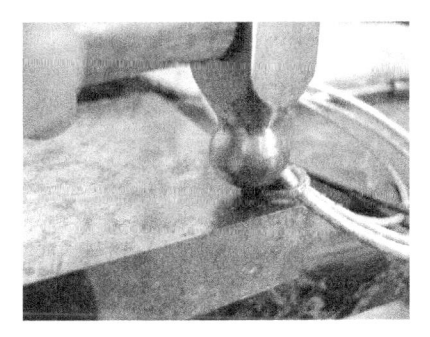

Step 9: Quench the entire piece, then clean the binding ring join. Hammer the sides once more if necessary.

Step 10: Pickle, rinse, and tumble polish the hammered three silver bangles to harden them further and give them an amazing shine.

How to Make Bangles

Pierce Metal Leaf Charm Bangle

Supplies

0.7mm copper sheet

5mm jump rings

3 silver tone bangles

Precious metal clay

Skeleton leaf

Tools

Handheld blow torch and firing brick

Scalpel

Acrylic rolling pin

Wire cutters

Ball peen hammer

Metal punch

Metal block

Wooden bench peg and G clamp

Saw frame and #3 blades

Metal burnisher

Double-sided tape

Coarse, medium, and fine emery papers

Pink carborundum

Needle files

5mm texturing attachment

Needle tool

A power tool with 2mm drill bit

Snipe-nosed, flat nosed, and round-nose pliers

Directions

Step 1: Cut out a template of an acorn, oak leaf, and medium leaf, ensuring to leave out a small border.

How to Make Bangles

Step 2: Using double-sided tape, attach the oak leaf template to a silver sheet and the acorn and medium leaf templates to a copper sheet.

Step 3: Cut the shapes and pierce them out, filing any rough saw marks and drilling holes for your jump rings.

Step 4: Create a mirror-like finish on the silver oak leaf and acorn using the emery papers.

Step 5: Texture the bottom half of the copper leaf and acorn with a texturing attachment and handheld power tool.

Step 6: Use the acrylic rolling pin to roll out a thin strip of silver clay. Lay the template of the oak leaf over the clay and cut it out. Press the skeleton leaf against the silver clay with the leaves running centrally.

Step 7: Remove the skeleton leaf, then create a tiny hole at the top using the needle tool.

Step 8: Use a needle file to neaten the leaf once completely dry.

Step 9: Place the clay design on a soldering block, then fire using the handheld blow torch. Cool in water.

Step 10: Use a wire brush to brush the leaf before washing it in liquid for a silver shine, then burnish. Attach the charms to the 6mm jump rings, then join them to your bangle.

TIP: You can also make a pair of earrings to match the bangle by using a jump ring to attach one small silver clay leaf and one large copper leaf to a large earing hoop.

How to Make Bangles

Metal Stamped Bangle Cuffs

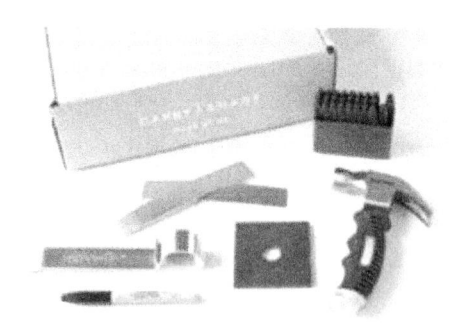

Supplies

Repoussé hammer

Permanent marker

Copper, silver, or brass metal sheet

Stamper and metal block

Directions

Step 1: Position your metal sheet over the metal block, then collect all letters you will require to make your message. You can begin stamping once you have your letters.

Step 2: Flip the alphabet stamp for your message to have the metal and the letter touching. Once you have the letter positioned where you like, hit the top of the stamp using the hammer provided in the kit. This may take you a few tries to get it just right, but there are some tips to make it easier:

*For the letter to get stamped evenly, you need to position the stamp straight up and down over the metal block. If you position it at an angle, some parts of the letter may not stamp out well. Also, ensure you hit the stamp only fairly hard for a nice depression.

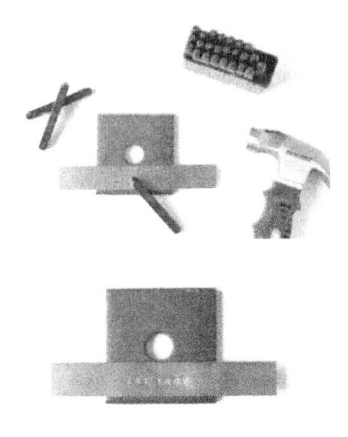

Step 3: After stamping your message onto the metal strip, the next thing is turning it into the shape of a bangle. Insert one end of your stamped metal sheet into the holder area/slit of the bracelet bending bar found in the kit. Create a curve by bending the other side downwards. Repeat the same for the other end of your metal strip. Your design should now have the basic shape of a bangle.

How to Make Bangles

Step 4: Make the finishing touches by running your permanent marker over the indentation made by the alphabet stamp and wiping off the excess immediately before it sets. The color of the marker remains in the indentations to make it easier to read the message stamped on the bangle cuff.

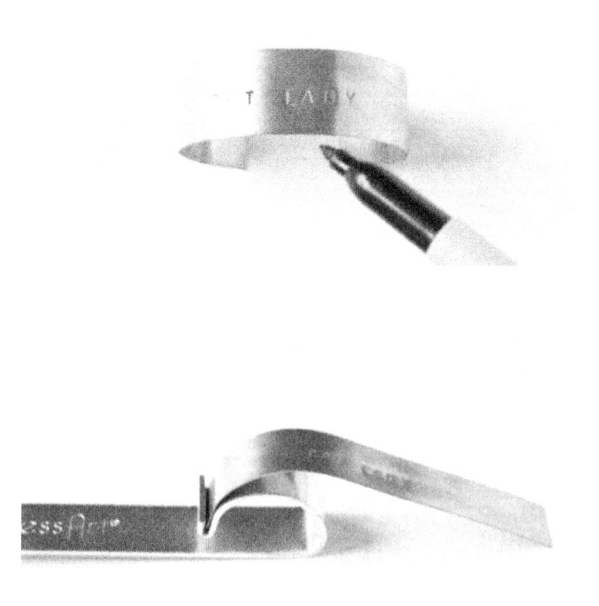

Boho Chic Rainbow Bangle Bracelets

Supplies

26 gauge gold wire

¼ - 3/8 inch wide satin ribbon in gold and bright rainbow colors – you'll need 30 inches for every bangle

Six 4mm Bicone crystals in rainbow colors

25-30 gold charms

30 thin plain metal bangles

Tools

Scissors

Round-nose pliers

Chain-nosed pliers

Wire cutters

How to Make Bangles

Beacon Fabri-tac glue

Directions

Step 1: Cut out a strip of ribbon measuring 30 inches long. Attach one end of your ribbon to 1 plain bangle. Twist the ribbon around the bangle until you slightly overlap the glued point. After wrapping the entire bangle, glue down the free end.

Step 2: To fix the charm, cut out a length of wire measuring 30 inches. Twist the wire approximately 30 times around the bangle wrapped with ribbon, leaving a 2-inch tail.

Use the round-nose pliers to create a loop for sliding on the charm. Complete the loop using two wraps, then trim the end neatly. Twist the tail from where the wire begins twice around the wrapped loop, then clip the end clean. Use pliers to press down on the freshly cut ends.

Step 3: To include the bicones, cut out a strip of wire measuring 30 inches. Leaving a 2-inch tail, twist the wire approximately three times around the bangle wrapped with ribbon.

Step 3: Slip bicones matching the ribbon into the wire, then twist the wire thrice again before adding another bicone.

Repeat the same process until your bangle has six bicones wrapped in the wire.

Step 4: Use the round-nose pliers to form a loop in the wire before sliding it on a charm. Complete the loop using two wraps, then trim the ends. Start twisting the tail from where the wire begins, twice around the wrapped loop, then clip the ends neat. Use pliers to press down the freshly cut ends.

How to Make Bangles

Chapter 5: Simple Woven Bangle Projects

Woven Bangle

Supplies

Low temp mini glue gun

75-yard raffia ribbon

4 glue sticks

Bead organizer and toolset

Loops & Threads ™ straight scissors

Hammered silver & gold matte round bangles

Charmalong ™ Dangling crystal charms

Directions

Step 1: Measure approximately 6 inches of raffia and cut it out. Locate the midpoint by folding it in half.

Step 2: Thread your bangles on one end of the raffia, sliding them up to the midpoint fold.

Step 3: Line up your bangle bracelets loop to loop to have an even raffia length on either side of the bangle.

Step 4: Grab the raffia on the right and twist it over the right side of your bangle before threading it through the center of the bangle, then position it to come out the left side.

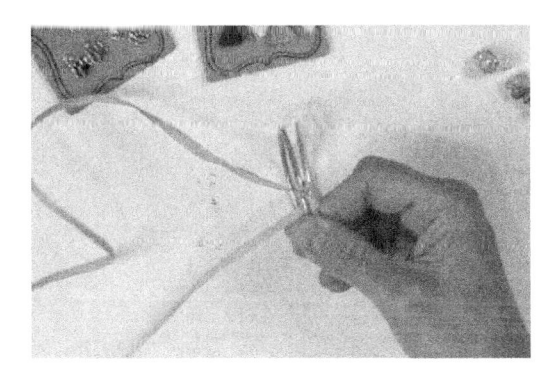

How to Make Bangles

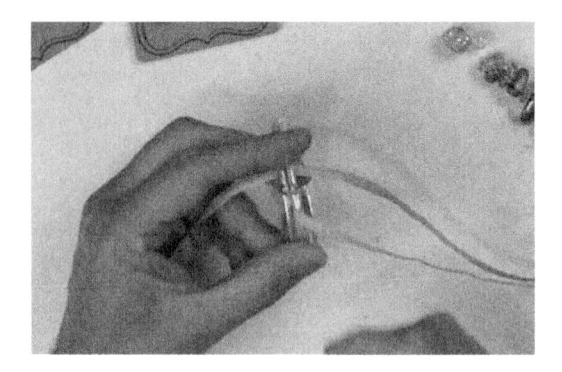

Step 5: Next, grab the raffia on the left, twist it over the left side of your bracelet before threading it through the center of the bangle, then position it to come out the right side. Yank the criss-crossed raffia taut.

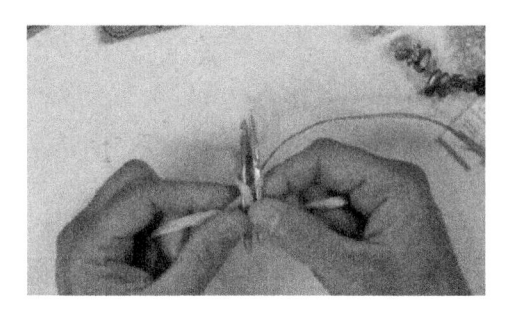

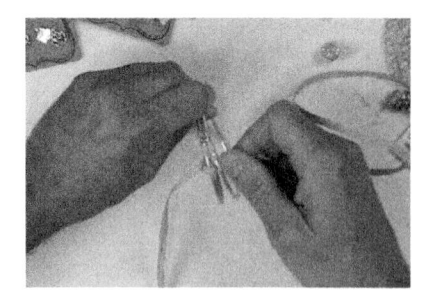

*The raffia that started on the right side is on the left and vice versa.

Step 5: Repeat step 4 until you have woven the raffia around the bangle.

Step 6: Wrap the ends around the loops in the shape of an X, then tie them into a knot under the bangle. Trim off the ends, then secure using hot glue.

Step 7: Add charms to the loops on your bangle using jump rings. To open and close the jump rings, just grab either side using a chain nose pliers and twist it side to side to open. Avoid pulling the jump rings as it can cause distortion.

How to Make Bangles

Woven Yarn Bangles

Supplies

Scissors

Glue

Basic bangles

3 colors of yarn

2 inches of wire

Directions

Step 1: Cut the yarn.

Cut the three colors of yarn to an equal length.

Step 2: Knotting and weaving

Grab one bangle and knot all three pieces onto it, ensuring the knot isn't so tight as you will have to remove it later u.

Grab another bangle and start weaving the yarn over and under between the two.

*You can continue weaving for a bit and proceed to the next step or try another technique as follows and then go to the next step.

Step 3: The other technique

This technique makes keeping your colors in the correct order easier and is faster once you get it.

Turn your bangle to have the side of yarn you'll be working with facing upward.

Using the hand on the same side as the already-woven part, position your thumb under the yarn as shown below:

Page | 67

How to Make Bangles

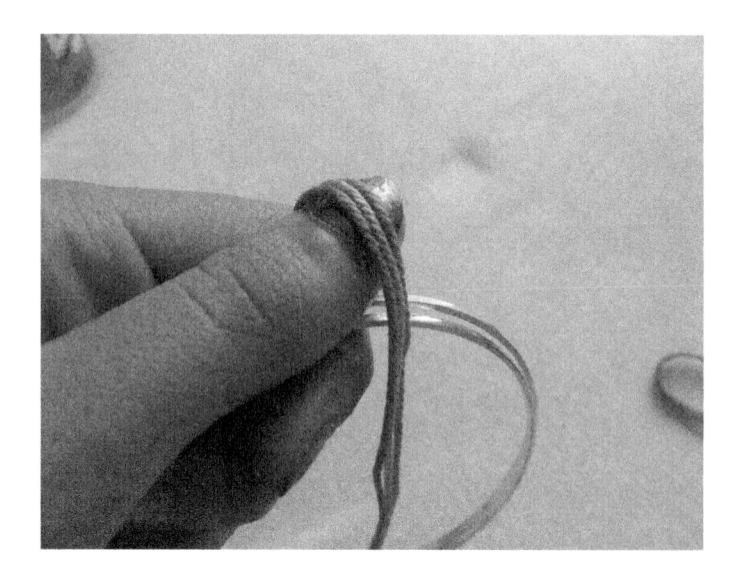

Ensuring your threads remain in the correct order, slip them in between the 2 bangles. Now yank the yarn through the 2 pieces of jewelry and remove your thumb. Pull taut.

Step 4: Work away from the starting point

After doing a bit of weaving, you now need to remove the knot at the beginning. After undoing the knot, apply glue underneath the yarn and start weaving in the same way as the other side of the bangle. Apply a generous amount of glue to the last part, tuck the yarn under the bangle, and trim off the excess.

Step 5: Continue weaving

Switch to the other side and continue weaving until only a couple of centimeters remain.

Step 6: Once nearly finished, apply glue under the yarn as you did when working away from the starting point. Since the space between your bangles has decreased significantly, it can be difficult to fit the yarn in between. Here's where the 2-

How to Make Bangles

inch wire comes in handy. Bend the wire to the shape of a U and use it as follows:

Step 7: When you reach the last part, apply plenty of glue and cut the yarn on the inside of your bangle for a more finished look like you did with the beginning.

Easy Woven Bangle Bracelet

Supplies

Ring connector

Jewelry glue

Glue on end caps and a clasp

6 strands of Cotton twine or hemp, 28 to 30 inches long – this project used Cotton.

Directions

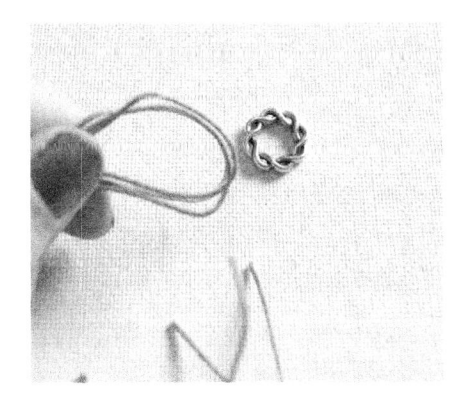

How to Make Bangles

Step 1: Grab 3 strands and fold them in half to form a loop at the center. Thread the loop through your ring connector.

Step 2: Attach the thread to the ring using a lark's head knot. If you are not familiar with how to make it, follow the steps below:

- Start by folding your strands in half to create a loop in the middle.

- Slip the looped cord end below the object.

- Grab the two ends of your cord and lead them upwards over the object and across the loop.

- Yank both ends until you have the loop tightly secured around the object.

This is how it will look once done:

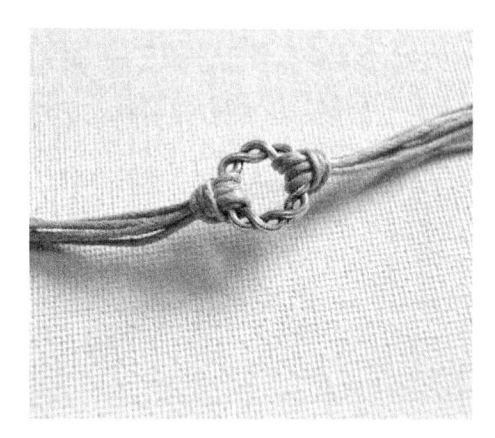

Step 3: Make the knot on either side of the ring such that you have 6 strings of around 13 to 14 inches long.

Step 4: Keeping the design simple, braid each side. If you like, you can form a 6-strand braid, but I used 2 cords in every strand for this project to make a regular braid.

Step 5: Once you reach the end, trim off your ends evenly, then apply some of the glue to your end cap before gluing it onto the freshly trimmed ends. Coat the twine fully by twisting around the end caps.

*TIP: Make sure you confirm the length of your piece against your wrist before you finish the ends off.

How to Make Bangles

Fun Accessory DIY Yarn Woven Bangles

Supplies

Scissors

Tapestry needle

Assorted yarn

Double-sided tape

Wooden bangle blanks – old, thrifted bangles work just fine too

Directions

Step 1: Use double-sided tape to line the inside of the bangle blank without peeling the backing layer.

Use the yarn color you'd like to have for the base to create a small ball that can fit through your bangle blank.

Step 2: Peel back a small section of the double-sided tape and thoroughly press down the end of your yarn.

Step 3: Cover the tail by wrapping your yarn around the bangle.

Step 4: Keeping the yarn close together, continue to wrap while peeling back the protective layer of the tape as you go.

How to Make Bangles

Adhere the yarn to the tape by firmly pressing it to the bangle.

Step 5: Finish by threading your needle with the remaining end and feet it underneath the securely wrapped yarn. Trim off the excess.

Step 6: Grab your tapestry needle and thread it with a strip of the contrasting yarn. Begin by sliding the needle under multiple wrapped strands on the bangle. The more strand you thread, the better secured the tail end will be.

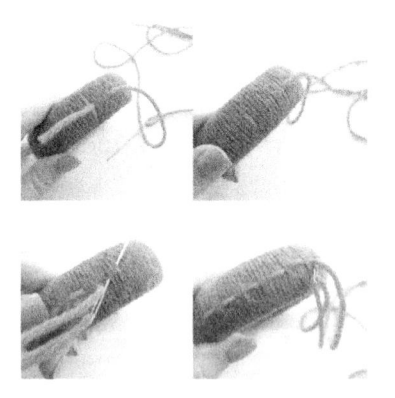

Step 7: Yank on the yarn until the tail end is out of sight.

Step 8: Weave in and out of the secured strands on your bangle to create your design.

Step 9: When you reach where you started, weave another row, this time switching in an in and out pattern a bit.

Step 10: Finish by feeding the tail end underneath the secured base yarn strips. Trim off the excess.

Chapter 6: Simple Wooden Bangle Projects

Wire Wrapped Wooden Bangle

Supplies

Wire cutters

Wire

Washi tape

Paintbrush

E6000 glue

Acrylic craft paint

Raw wood bangle bracelet

Directions

Step 1: Wrap the washi tape around half the surface of your bangle. Line the corresponding half inside your bangle as well. Although the multiple curved surfaces of the bracelet make it impossible for the tape to lie completely flat, try smoothing it down as much as possible.

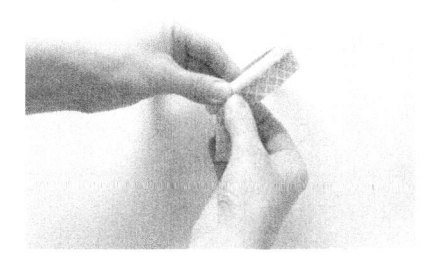

Step 2: Use a small paintbrush to paint the exposed section of your bracelet. You can use any color you like, but it's best to pick a color with a nice contrast to the wire and the wood. Give the bangle a couple of hours to dry off, then peel off the tape gently.

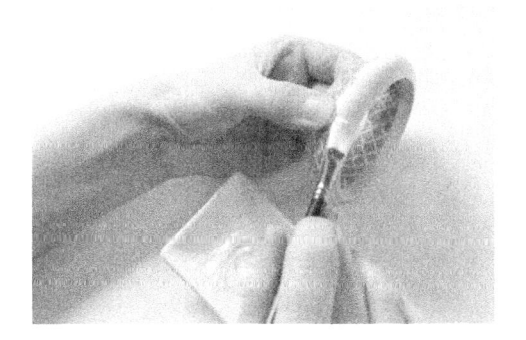

Step 3: Start to wrap the wire around the bangle, ensuring you push each coil right next to the last one and pull as tight as possible. This ensures you don't have huge gaps between

How to Make Bangles

the wire strand coils. Wrap approximately 3 inches.

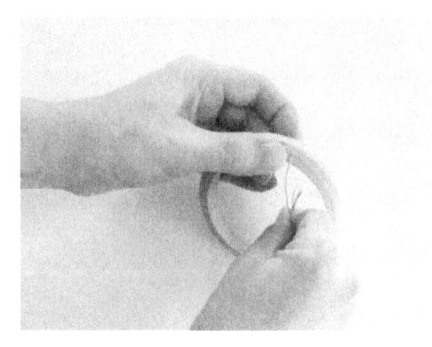

*If your wire runs out before you can complete the pattern, trim the end on the inside of your bangle and begin a fresh piece.

Step 4: Use the E6000 glue to secure the ends so that they are not poking at your wrist when you wear them. If the ends are still stubborn, wait for the E6000 to dry, then add some super glue and hold the wires in place till it dries up.

Painted Wooden Bangles

Supplies

Wood stain

Wooden bangle blank

Washi tape

Craft paint

Gloss finish

Foam brush for applying stain

Small paintbrush

Soft paint brush for applying the gloss finish

Directions

How to Make Bangles

Step 1: Brushing in your wood grain direction, apply the wood stain all over the wooden blank using the foam brush. This can get a messy, but you can easily get the wood stain off using nail polish remover.

Remove the excess stain using paper towels and allow it to sit for an hour. (Or according to the manufacturer's instructions on the stain you are using)

Step 2: Make stencils on the stained bangle using washi tape, pressing the edges firmly onto the wood, and smooth it out. You can make your stencil design vertically, horizontally, or randomly.

*If you want to make a color-blocked bangle, ensure you avoid painting towards the edge of the tape to keep the paint from seeping, but if it still does, you can scrape away the excess paint carefully using your nail.

Step 3: Paint your taped bangle. You will probably have to apply around 2-3 coats for a solid color. If you get impatient between the coats, you can try drying the paint quickly using a hair dryer.

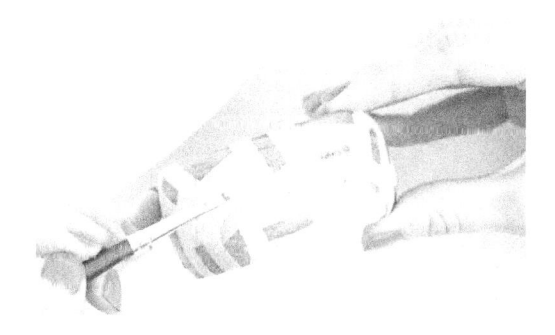

Once you apply the last coat, give the paint a couple of seconds and remove the tape carefully before it dries. Then you can now leave the paint to dry completely.

Step 4: Use the soft paintbrush to apply the gloss finish for the final step. This will help keep the paint from chipping and give your piece of jewelry a nice clean sheen.

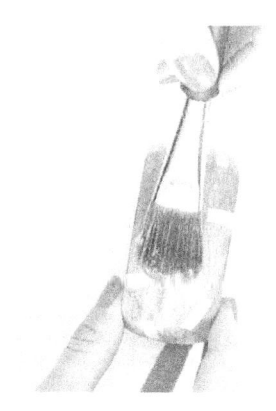

How to Make Bangles

*You can also paint your bangle using the polka dot pattern. Simply use a 1/8 inch hole punch to punch holes into a stencil material in a polka dot pattern, then place it on the bangle and paint the same way as we did on this project.

Wooden Bangles For Animal Lovers

Supplies

Acrylic, tempera or gouache paint

1 inch wide blank wooden bangles

Optional: Ink pens to make fine details – try working with size 01 Copic inking pens or Sakura ink pens

Varnish – if using acrylic paint, you can work with any acrylic varnish, but I used DecoArt Triple Thick Gloss Glaze. If using tempera or gouache, ensure you use a non-water-based varnish, though I recommend using Golden MSA Varnish specifically for the white bangle as it doesn't yellow.

Directions

Step 1: Apply the base coat on your bangle blank using your preferred paint. For a smooth finish, use a paintbrush – I did this for the black bangle. If you prefer an eggshell texture, use a sponge – I did this for the white bangle.

How to Make Bangles

Step 2: Wait until the paint has dried and draw on it the facial features of your preferred animal with a pencil – I went with a cat and an eagle. You can avoid unwanted permanent marks by ensuring the pencil is soft, and the paint is thoroughly dry.

Step 3: Gather the paints and brushes for the facial features —for both designs, you need black, white, ochre, yellow, and blue paint. For the brushes, get the small round ones suitable for making fine details.

Step 4: Start painting. Use the yellow paint to fill the eye spaces and lightly mark the silhouette of the animal faces. Allow the paint to dry off completely, then use an eraser to erase any visible pencil marks.

Step 5: Highlight the eyes and draw the pupils inside them using an ink pen or a small round brush. For the final touch, paint white highlights around the eyes.

Step 6: Apply varnish to give your bangle a glossy finish.

DIY Mod Podge Wood Bangle Bracelets

Supplies

Paintbrush

Paper or graphic of your choice – you'll need to cut it evenly using a paper trimmer

Mod podge

Acrylic paint

Flat wooden bangle bracelets

Directions

Step 1: Begin by trimming the paper to your bangle's width. Paint the edges and inside of the bracelet. You can also paint the outside of your piece just for fun or if your paper is slightly short.

How to Make Bangles

Step 2: Apply some mod podge behind the paper, then press it on the outside of your bangle. Straighten and smoothen the paper before covering it with mod podge. Allow it to dry.

Once dry, coat the edges and inside the bracelets with mod podge, then smooth out any smudges. Allow it to dry.

Chapter 7: Simple Fabric Bangle Projects

No-Sew Simple Fabric Bangle Bracelet

Supplies

Hot glue

Lollipop sticks

Fish tank tubing

Fabric strips – this project used bandanas

Directions

Step 1: Cut out your fabric into 1-inch strands. Trim off the strings.

How to Make Bangles

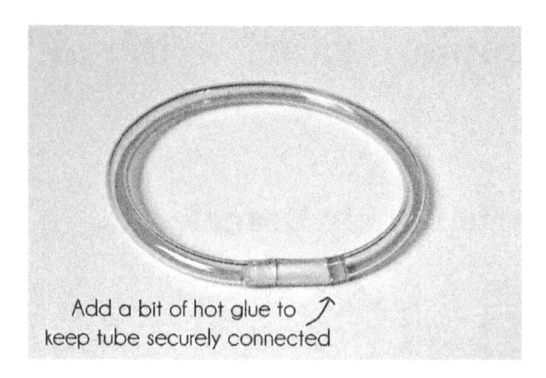

Add a bit of hot glue to keep tube securely connected

Step 2: Cut the fish tank tubing to fit the wrist of the wearer. Clip the lollipop stick into smaller pieces. Apply some hot glue inside one end of your tubing, then slide one piece of the lollipop stick in. Apply some more glue on the remaining end and slip it into the other tubing end. This forms a circle.

Step 3: Secure the fabric to the tube by adding some hot glue at the beginning of the wrap. Begin wrapping the fabric around the tube and even twisting if necessary.

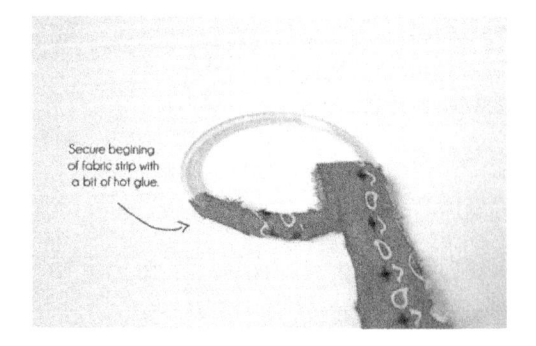

Secure beginning of fabric strip with a bit of hot glue.

Step 4: Continue wrapping until you cover the whole tube. One strip from a bandana is 22 inches long and only covers the bangle size of a small child. If your fabric runs out before completing this process, attach another strip using a bit of glue.

*Tip: Wrap a bit more around the beginning of the new strip to conceal any seams. Also, ensure you keep the fabric as tight as possible when wrapping.

Once you come to an end, secure the end with glue and trim off the extra fabric.

How to Make Bangles

Quick And Easy DIY Fabric Bangle

Supplies

Fabric

Scissors

Fabric glue

Iron

Plain metal or plastic bangles

Directions

Step 1: Measure and cut

Start by cutting a strip of fabric that is 4 inches in width. Now cut the 4-inch strand lengthwise in half to have 2 strips measuring 2 inches long.

2" wide

Step 2: Fold and iron

Fold in half an inch on either long edge, then iron to keep the fold in place.

Step 3: Apply glue

Apply some glue to one end of the strip of fabric and the inside folds of your piece to secure firmly.

Step 4: Attach fabric

Press the glued end of your fabric on the inner side of the bracelet.

Step 5: Glue and wrap

Once the fabric end is secured and dry, apply more glue to the bangle and begin to wrap the fabric around it. Continue until you have covered the entire bracelet with fabric.

How to Make Bangles

Step 6: Cut

Once you have wrapped the whole bracelet, trim off the frayed ends.

Step 7: Glue the end

Apply plenty of glue to the fabric's end, ensuring to get in between the folds as you did before. Hide the raw edge by folding the end inwards approximately 0.5 inches, then glue it to the inside of your bangle.

DIY Bangle From Fabric And Hanger

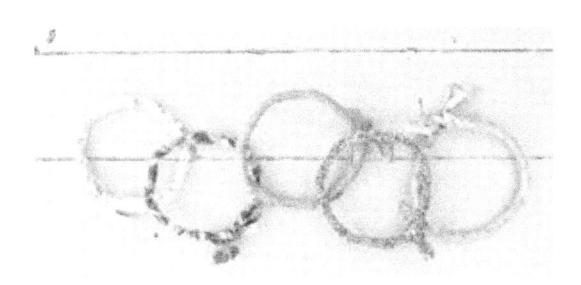

Supplies

Scissors

Wire cutters

1 yard of fabric strip (approximately 1 inch wide)

Thin wire hanger or an 18 gauge floral wire

Directions

Step 1: Cut off the base of the hanger using your wire cutters. Just use floral wire if you have trouble bending or cutting the hanger. (The thinner your hanger, the easier it is to cut.)

Step 2: Create a round bangle shape by bending the wire, then tuck away the ends. If bending the ends by hand proves difficult, you can help bend them using wire cutters.

How to Make Bangles

Step 3: Tie one end of the fabric strip onto the bangle in a simple knot, which will leave you with a tail approximately 2 inches long.

Step 4: Start wrapping the bangle using the longer end until you have covered all the wire.

Step 5: Tie the remaining tail of your fabric to the initial knot, then clip off the extra.

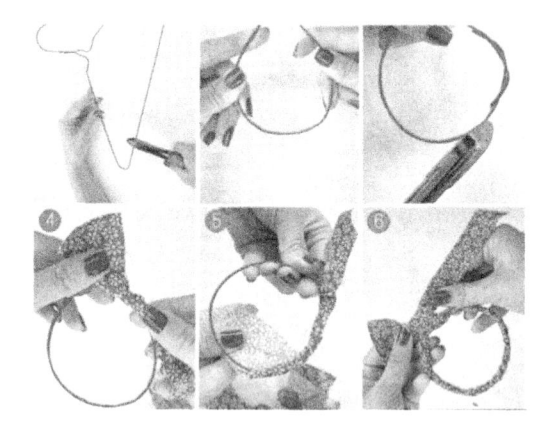

Upcycle Scrap Fabric into Wrapped Bangles

Supplies

Scissors

Old bangle bracelets

Long fabric scraps 1-2cm in width – the length can vary

Optional

Washi tape

Needle and thread

Directions

Step 1: Cut out the fabric strips

Cut or tear out strips of fabric 2 cm in width from an old shirt. You can keep the length of the fabric depending on

How to Make Bangles

where you are cutting it from —the sleeve or front of the shirt. You don't have to worry about the length; work with what you have —If your strips are too short, you can add a second strip and if they are too long, simply trim it short at the end.

Step 2: Attaching the fabric strip

Use washi tape, plain cello tape, or a dab of hot glue to secure the fabric to your bangle for the first couple of wraps. (I used washi tape for this project). This simply keeps your fabric from slipping away while wrapping the bangle.

Step 3: Wrapping the fabric

Now wrap the fabric around the bangle, overlapping the fabric a bit after every turn and pulling as tight as possible as you go.

Continue wrapping until there's no sight of the initial bangle, but not too much that the bangle becomes too heavy and thick with multiple fabric layers.

Step 4: Make a bow or sew the end

The first option to finish the bangle is to trim the excess tail once you reach where you began, turn the end of the strip to face downwards, then stitch it in place. If the remaining fabric tail is still long, you can create a knot and form a bow embellishment instead of trimming. To make the bow, cut the length of the fabric left in half after tying your knot. Create the bow using the two strips.

*You can try making more bangles with different strip widths and fabric colors or include other embellishments such as bits, ribbons, or buttons for unique designs.

Chapter 7: Other Simple Bangle Projects

DIY Criss Cross Leather And Chain Bangle

Supplies

2 strands of curb chain

2 Leather cords – I used purple and black for this project

16-18 gauge flat aluminum craft wire

3-in-1 jewelry pliers

Scissors

Clear nail polish

Super glue

Tin can or mason jar

Optional: Masking tape

Directions

Step 1: Cut out a strip of flat wire to be your wrist length plus an additional 6 to 8 inches.

Step 2: Cut 2 strips of leather cord, each measuring approximately 20 inches in length. Tightly secure each strand close to one end of your wire using a knot. Grab and thread the first link of one of your chains through the black or purple cord.

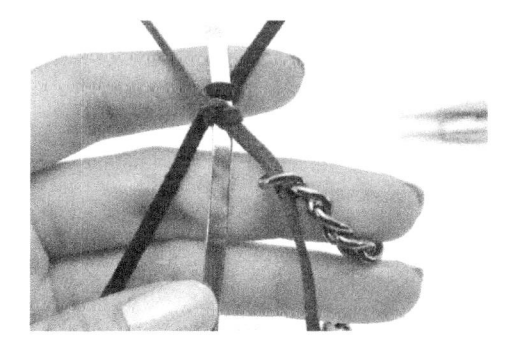

Step 3: Next, thread the first link of your second chain through the cord on the other side.

How to Make Bangles

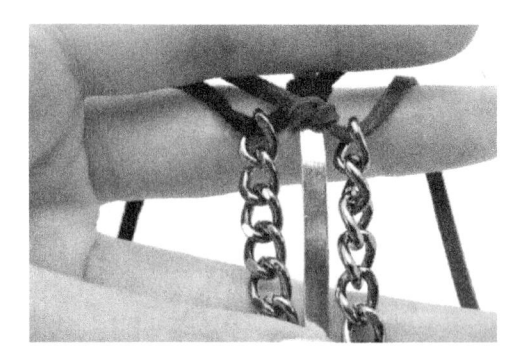

Step 4: With the chains parallel to the wire and laying flat, grab the right-side cord and lead it to the left of your wire, sliding it through the left chain's second link as shown below:

Step 5: Now grab the left side cord and bring it to the right of the wire, threading it through the right chain's second link. This way, the black and purple cords switch sides, with the black becoming the "new" right strand and the purple becoming the "new" left strand.

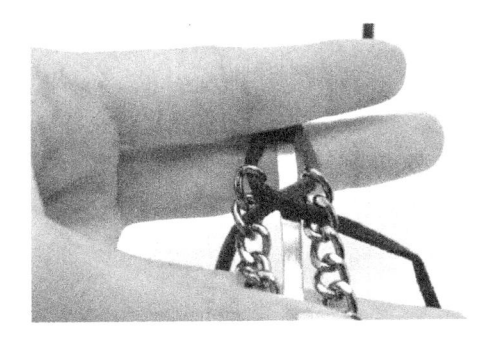

Step 6: Grab either leather cord and criss-cross them under the wire. The black cord will go under the wire, then below, and through the third link on the left chain, whereas the purple cord goes under the wire, then below, and through the third link on the right-side chain. The two leather cords criss-cross underneath the wire.

Step 7: Repeat the same process where, now, the purple cord crosses the wire to the left, then threads through the left chain's fourth link while the black cord goes over the wire to the right side and inserts into the right chain's fourth link. Repeat until you come to the end of your chain.

How to Make Bangles

Step 8: Finish the end by tying a secure triple knot and trimming off the excess cord.

Step 9: Go to the other end where you began and create another triple knot, trimming the excess off.

Step 10: Trim off the excess wire on either end, then finish each end by bending it into a loop.

Step 11: Wrap the bangle around a tin can or mason jar to help shape it.

Optional

- For extra security, apply a few nail polish dots to your knots.

- You can also use a pointed tip applicator (if readily available) to apply a few dots of super glue between the leather cord and wire for additional security.

How to Make Bangles

DIY Dainty Washer Bracelet

Supplies

Strips of fabric or ribbon cut into ¼-1 inch thick pieces

Line paper

Tape

Clear top coat

Nail polish

Washers

Cutting board

Directions

Step 1: To begin, lay your line paper over the cutting board, then select a color palette.

Step 2: Choose your preferred pattern and leave a space of one line apart between the washers.

Step 3: With the washers still on the line paper, start painting their edges, moving to the top surface. You will need to apply 3-4 coats for a solid color.

TIP: Begin with thin, even coats like when painting your nails and allow the polish enough time to dry between coats. If you get impatient waiting, you can dry it faster using a hair dryer instead of filling on the polish in a single sweep.

Step 4: Paint the remaining washers and finish with a clear top coat. Allow the washers to dry thoroughly before flipping

How to Make Bangles

over and repeating the same process on the other side. (You can try speeding up the process using Sally Hansen Dries Instantly Top Coat.)

Step 5: Wrap the ribbon around your wrist to fit the size and add an extra 4-5 inches. Trim the excess ribbon off.

Step 6: Grab your ribbon length, position it at the edge of your tape, and wrap it as tight as possible.

The end of the ribbon should look as shown below once done:

Step 7: Thread the washer through the needle formed at the end of your ribbon until you are 4-5 inches from the other end.

Step 8: Slide another washer through the ribbon, leaving a finger width space with the first washer as shown below:

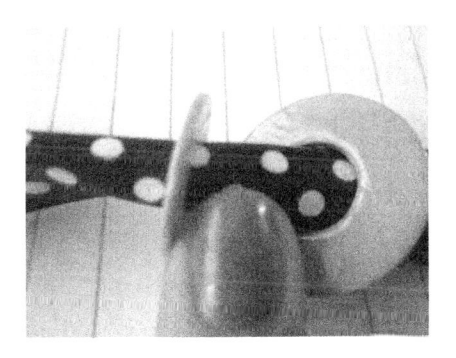

Step 9: Feed the needle of your ribbon through the middle of the initial washer, going entirely over your second washer. Make sure the ribbon remains even and flat.

Step 10: While looping the 'needle' back around, insert it through the middle of the second washer, thus forming a figure 8 shape.

How to Make Bangles

Step 11: Secure the washers by yanking tightly on either end of your ribbon. It will look something like this:

Rework steps 8 to 11. Remember that we thread the needle through the middle of the last washer and then loop it back to the next washer.

*You can use multiple ribbons and switch out the colors.

Harlequin Decoupage Bangle

Supplies

Paintbrush

Medium/fine sandpaper

Small dish

Mod podge or PVA (wood) glue

Scissors

Assorted colors of Origami paper

Wooden bangle blank

2 tins

Wooden skewer

Ruler

Protected surface

How to Make Bangles

Pencil

Directions

Step 1: Use sandpaper to smooth — lightly— any rough edges on your bangle blank.

Step 2: Measure your bangle's width, then sketch diamond shapes behind the origami paper.

Step 3: Cut out the diamond and triangular shapes sketched on your paper.

Step 4: Lay out the origami pieces and measure your bangle's circumference to ensure they fit nicely. Slightly trim your shapes if they are too long until they fit together well.

measure circumference

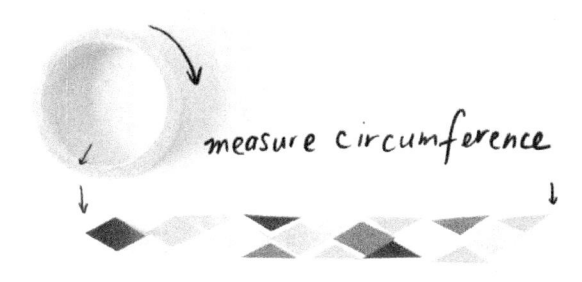

Step 5: Add a small amount of mod podge or glue into the small dish.

Step 6: Brush the outer surface of your bangle with the glue, then begin to stick on the paper shapes.

Step 7: Brush the top of your paper shapes with glue as you continue sticking them onto the bangle. Don't be alarmed by the white layer left behind when applying the glue, as it will become shiny and clear once dry.

How to Make Bangles

Step 8: Thread your wooden skewer through the bangle, then balance it between 2 tins to dry up. Allow the glue to dry until it turns clear.

Step 9: Finish the inside and edges of the bracelet by coating with mod podge or diluted glue mixture. If using PVA glue, slightly thin it out by watering it down with one tablespoon of water. No thinning is required if using mod podge.

Step 10: Allow the first coat to dry thoroughly, then add another coating or 2 all over the whole bangle.

Coral And Sea Shell Resin Bangles

Supplies

Bangle bracelet resin mold – ensure its specially designed for casting resin

Mold release conditioner spray – to ensure bangles don't get stuck in the mold permanently.

Small sea shells/coral pieces

Clear casting resin (usually comes with resin catalyst)

Disposable cups – to mix the resin

Transparent resin dye – for adding color to the bangles

Cardboard or newspaper for protection of your workspace as resin can get quite messy

Directions

How to Make Bangles

Step 1: Add the resin catalyst and casting resin to the disposable cup and mix. Slowly stir the mixture to avoid forming extra bubbles (most bubbles disappear once the resin sets); however, ensure you stir thoroughly until there are no swirls left. If you don't stir the mixture sufficiently, it will not set.

Step 2: Add your resin mix to the bangle mold until it's halfway filled and allow it to set. (The setting time varies according to the brand you use, but mine took around 1 hour).

Step 3: Lay out the coral pieces and sea shells on your working surface to determine your preferred pattern because once you place them in the resin, they will get stuck, making it impossible to adjust their position.

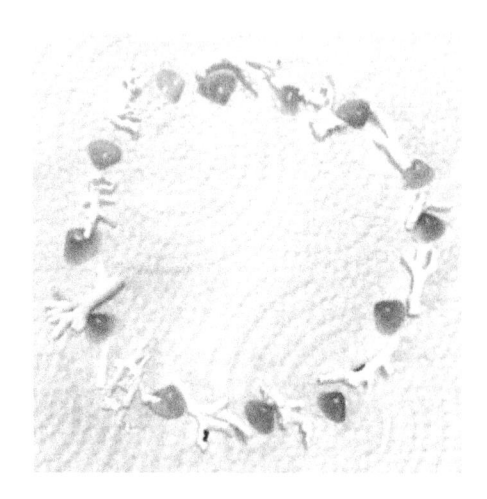

Step 4: Add the coral and seashells to the resin in your desired pattern once it sets. Give the shells 30-60 minutes to set in the resin.

Step 5: Mix up another resin batch, then add to the mold to top up the other half. Ensure the resin is thoroughly dry before trying to remove the bangle from the mold. Mine took about 24 hours.

*You can make more bangles of different colors using different resin dyes.

How to Make Bangles

DIY Zipper Bangle Bracelets

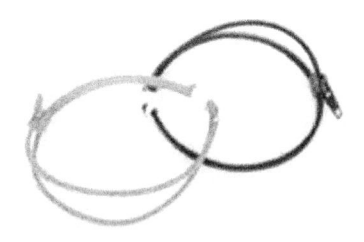

Supplies

Embroidery needle

Embroidery floss

Fabric scissors

Clear or contrasting nail polish

Cheap colorful 9-inch zippers

Directions

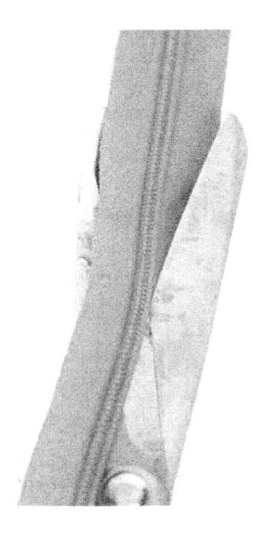

Step 1: Trim off the fabric from your zipper along the zipper's edge. To avoid fraying, finish the edges with coordinating or clear nail polish.

Step 2: Measure the length of the zipper against your wrist, leaving enough space to slip it on.

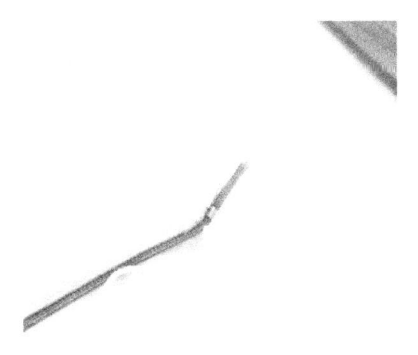

How to Make Bangles

Step 3: Now sew the ends together. Thread your needle with embroidery floss, then stick it through the middle of the zipper.

Step 4: Join both ends of the same strip, then stick the needle through to the other side as shown below:

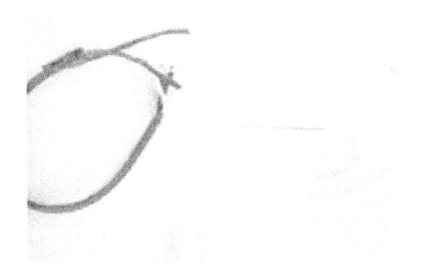

Step 5: Wrap the thread around both ends until nice and secure; then, you can thread the needle back through the center of the zipper. Secure in place with a knot.

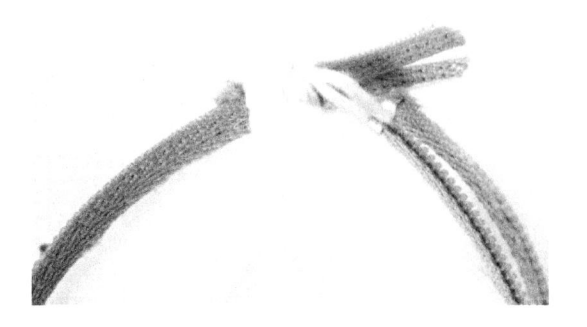

Step 6: Finish by trimming off the excess zipper.

How To Make Thread Bangles

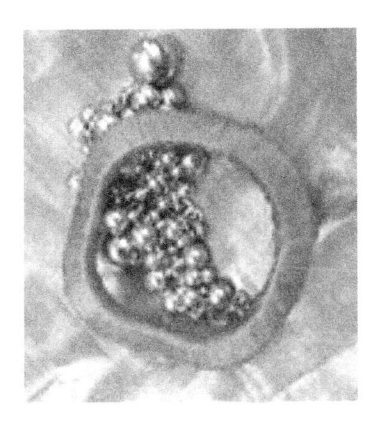

Supplies

Scissors

Old bangles of any shape – I used a plastic wavy old bangle

Assorted colors of silk thread

Directions

Step 1: Begin by cleaning the bangle thoroughly to remove any dust or oils.

Step 2: Grab 5-6 thread strings in your hand that are approximately 30cm long. If the strings are too long, working with them becomes more challenging.

*Working with 5-6 strands at a go speeds up the wrapping, which saves on energy and time.

How to Make Bangles

Step3: Wrap the strings around your bangle multiple times in the same direction. Ensure you do it in an organized manner such that the strands are all nice, straight, and close together; otherwise, the bangle will look rather unattractive.

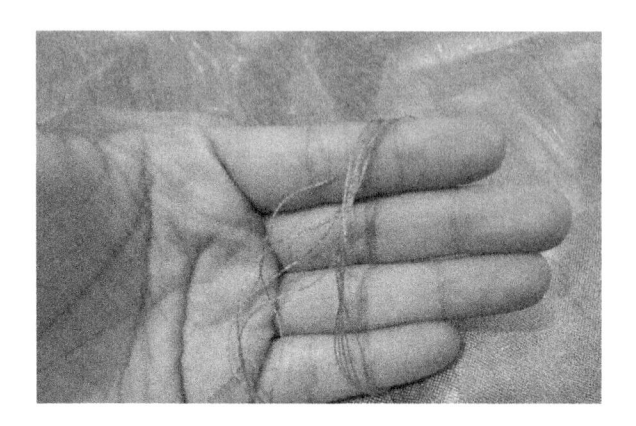

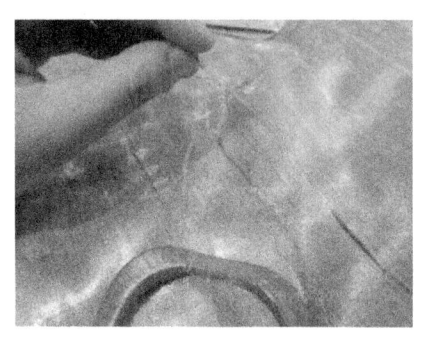

Step 4: Once you run out of the first batch of strings, connect the loose ends with the new batch of strings using a knot. Trim off the excess. The soft nature of silk increases the chances of the thread slipping away, so ensure you fasten the knot tight and secure. Ensure the knot is inside the bangle too.

Step 5: From here, you can continue wrapping the strands around the bangle, keeping them lined up, and when the string runs out, attach the fresh batch using another knot – inside the bangle.

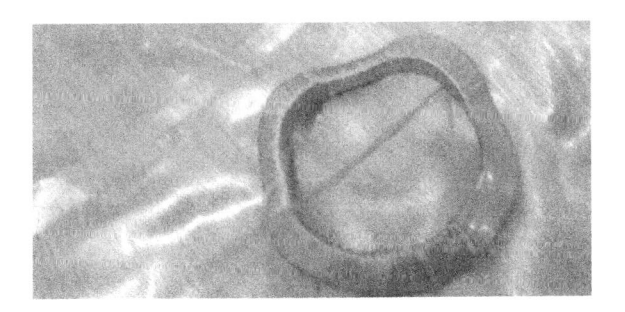

Step 6: Keep twisting the strands until the whole bangle is completely covered.

*You can wrap the other bangles the same way using different colors of threads or make a multicolored bracelet.

How to Make Bangles

Easy-to-Make Delicate Beaded Bangles

Supplies

1.3mm gold crimp beads, size 01

2mm gold seed beads

5mm and 2mm x 3mm faceted crystal beads

65 diameter gold memory wire

Wire cutters

Round-nose pliers

Chain-nose pliers

Directions

Step 1: Start by cutting out a single memory wire coil plus an overlap of 1\2 inches. Memory wire is a hard, permanently coiled wire. This type of wire has "memory" where it can bounce back to its initial shape after being distorted.

*Because memory wire is very hard, I do not advise using your good wire cutters. You can find or borrow an old pair.

Step 2: Thread one crimp bead through the wire but don't crimp it just yet. This bead bites into the wire when crimped and acts as a stopper for beads. We will add a crimp bead on either side of the other beads to keep them in the middle of the bracelet.

Step 3: Slide 5 gold seed beads across the wire.

Step 4: Insert 1 faceted crystal bead into the wire.

Step 5: Feed 5 more gold seed beads through the wire.

Step 6: Add 1 crimp bead to have the other beads sandwiched between 2 crimp beads. Don't crimp the bead.

Step 7: Make the bangle closure using the round-nose pliers to grip the end of your memory wire. Bend a loop on your wire end by rotating the pliers —as mentioned earlier, this

How to Make Bangles

wire is very hard. You will need a bit of elbow grease for this step.

Step 8: Flip over your bangle and create another loop on the other end of the wire coil using the same process.

Step 9: Using the chain-nose pliers, grab one loop and bend it to 90 degrees.

Step 10: Bend the other loop on the other end to a right angle. Both loops will now face each other.

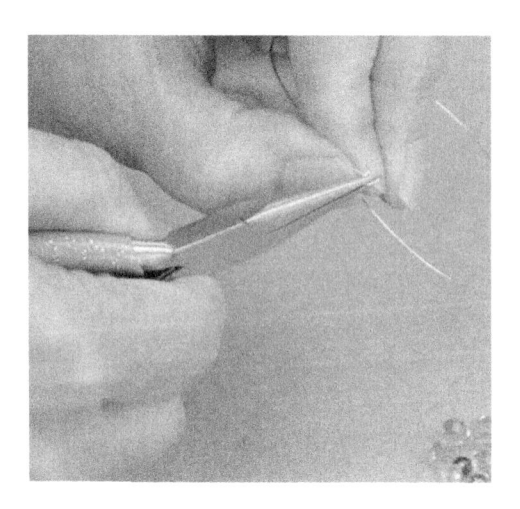

Step 11: Open one loop enough to insert the bangle wire through it.

Step 12: Slide the wire through the loop, then press it closed.

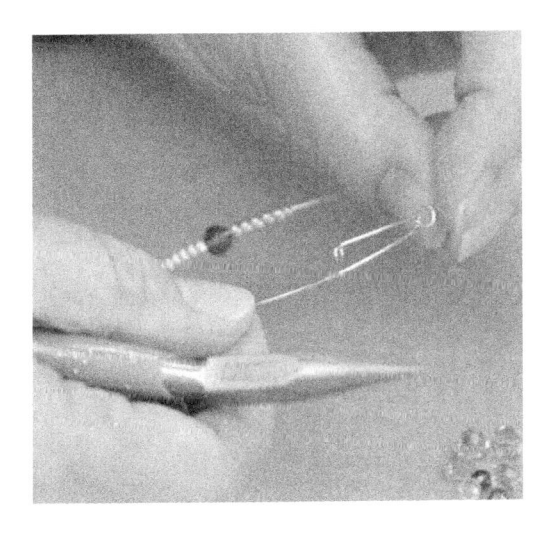

Repeat the same process for the other loop to have the bangle wire running through either loop.

Step 13: Center your beads on the bracelet opposite the closure, then use your chain-nose pliers to press one crimp bead flat onto the wire.

How to Make Bangles

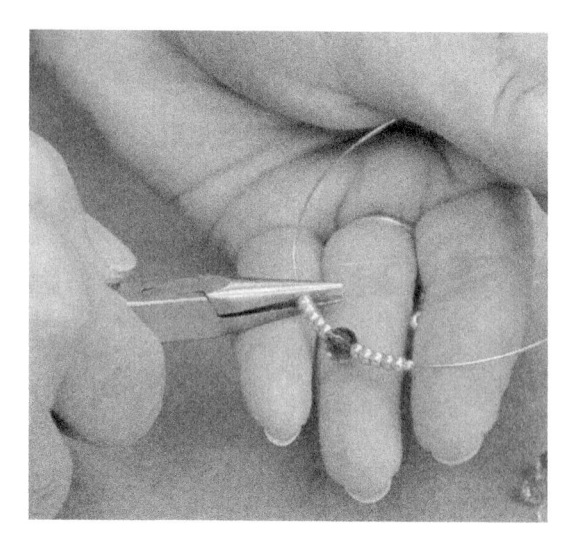

Step 14: Push your beads together, then press the other crimp bead flat onto the wire in the same way.

Chapter 8: Where To Begin

Now that you have all the basics and multiple simple projects to try out, it's time to get to the practical stuff. If you're new to the bangle-making craft, you are probably wondering where to begin. This chapter has you covered. The steps below will ease you into creating personalized bangle designs:

Step 1: Search for inspiration

You first need to get inspired: you can visit jewelry stores or check out the endless possibilities online. As you do this, also determine the type of materials you'd prefer working with, be it glass, metal, or clay.

Step 2: Design your piece

If you don't know or are unsure where to start, you can begin sketching your design on paper. Consider the different materials, colors, and shapes that inspire you. You can draw inspiration from a vintage piece or create your own design from scratch.

As you sketch, it helps you determine the tools and types of materials you'll require to bring life to your drawing. When designing your piece, label the parts of your sketch with the needed materials.

Step 3: Acquire the materials and tools

Once you come up with a design, what follows is to collect the tools and materials you will require to turn your design into reality. For example, you will need soldering equipment and a torch to create soldered bangles using precious metals. A kiln is necessary if you have more advanced equipment and are interested in metal clay bangles or fused glass bangles. You'll need a centrifugal casting machine if your project requires casting precious metals.

Step 4: Set up your workspace

Find a place with plenty of light and set up a clean table. Get a sturdy workbench that doesn't wobble when you stamp, hammer, and work the bangle. Since you may end up sitting for a couple of hours while working on the piece of jewelry, it's a good idea to get a comfortable seat. Look for a chair that will support your neck and back. The bench peg and your seat should be at eye level to help you avoid hunching over your work. If you intend to do any polishing, soldering, or sanding, ensure you have adequate ventilation and proper fire safety equipment, a mask, and safety goggles.

Step 5: Start making

After planning out your design, gathering the necessary materials, and setting up your workspace, all that's left is to begin creating your project.

Before slipping on the bangles:

It is essential to realize that putting on bangles involves more than just sliding them up your wrist. There are significant factors you need to consider to avoid a tacky look, and these factors include:

Size

There are many sizes of bangles to account for the different sizes of people's wrists.

The first and perhaps the most obvious thing you should do is ensure that your bangles are not too small or too big for you. The bangle should be fitted enough not to slip off and loose enough not to squeeze your wrist.

Additionally, if you wear multiple bangles, ensure you pick consistent sizes; otherwise, the smaller bangles may get stuck in the larger ones and wind up deformed.

Color

How to Make Bangles

To give your bangle game an epic edge over others, you must know how to contrast and layer the colors. Bangles are available in a wide range of colors that you can blend in a gorgeous and unique style; it all depends on your taste. If you like monochrome, you can acquire the same shade of bangle color—it usually comes in sets.

Mood

The mood depends on the occasion where you'll be wearing the bangles to. Whether you want a set of multiple bangles stacked on your wrist or one large bangle, the "to where" matters a lot.

It is typical to accessorize formal outfits minimally, so you may want to go for a bunch of bangles that are not colored too brightly or a single bangle. For more informal occasions, you can choose your bangles based on personal taste.

Texture

As discussed in earlier chapters of the books, we can make bangles from different types of materials, so don't be boring.

You can make things interesting by mixing up leather bangles with animal print and some metal. Mixing the bangle texture makes a profound impression on almost any outfit you pick out. You can do both hands or one and throw in a few worded bangles.

Charms

Most charms have a special significance to the people wearing them; they also give bangles a gorgeous look. Charm bangles are usually more snug compared to regular bangles. However, if you are all for details, they will make an impression on you. Add charms to personalize your bangles and signify something special to you.

*You can also try wearing ankle bangles; adorning your ankles is almost as important as adorning your wrists. Besides, who said you could only put bangles on your hands?

Helpful Tips On How To Style Your Bangles

Once you have created your bangle bracelets, the best part comes: styling them into your outfit! There's a way you can wear your bangles, and instead of complimenting your style, they make you look ridiculous and unflattering no matter how gorgeous the bracelets themselves are. Each outfit you wear will determine the appropriate bangle color pick, how many bangles you wear, how to mix up different bangles stylishly, and so much more. The tips below will help you get the most out of your bangle bracelets:

Mix and match

Mixing and matching your bangles makes your jewelry stand out. We can achieve this by incorporating different bangle styles on your wrists. However, if you are unsure of where to start, begin with the basics: wear 3-4 bangles with shared qualities.

You can wear different bangles with similar traits and shuffle them based on your outfit. For instance, you can put on a string bangle with custom silicone wristbands or stack it on gold bangles. Although, if you are feeling creative, you can try varying the color and width of the bangles throughout your wrist.

When picking out the bracelets, ensure they complement each other. When one piece contrasts another, the entire stack looks odd and uncomplimentary.

Sometimes less is more

While it can be fun and creative to stack heavy bangles, sometimes it may be uncalled for. Simplicity is sometimes better than excessively accessorizing, especially in a formal setting. Avoid stacking a lot of bracelets at once. Instead, you could keep a maximum of 3-4 bangles in each arm.

Wearing chunky jewelry may be fun. However, when you overdo it, it can make your outfit seem chaotic instead of fashionable. A dainty silver bracelet or simple leather bangle band will do just fine. You may be surprised by how much a thin bangle bracelet can improve your look.

Do not mix metals

Mixing and matching usually work, but it is not always the case with metal types. You have to be very careful when mixing metal jewelry. Otherwise, you may end up looking very unflattering.

Bangles made of gold, sterling silver, and platinum are all spectacular, but it doesn't necessarily mean they go together. Of course, unless the bangle itself is made of mixed metal types. In such a case, you can try mixing up the metals and see how it looks, whether it's up to your style.

However, it is generally best to wear only one metal type. For instance, you can match a few silver bangles with other jewelry made of silver metals to coordinate with your outfit.

Consider your sleeve length

Considering the length of your sleeves is very important but often overlooked. If you intend to put on a long-sleeved dress, there's no need to wear a few bracelets that nobody will see – you can opt for a large pair of earrings or a long necklace instead.

Bangles go well with shorter sleeves or sleeveless outfits where they are exposed, and you can show them off. Long sleeves tend to hide bangles, but with short sleeve outfits, they can become the prime focus. Therefore it's important to select clothes that you can pair well with bracelets if you must put them on.

Conclusion

We have come to the end of the book, which is very exciting as you can now venture into making bangles, and, at this point in the guidebook, you have all you need to get into this craft.

As mentioned in the early chapters of the book, we have three main classifications of bangles: according to their structure, their base material, and style. So, before you begin, you will have to decide whether you want to make cuff bangles, split cylinder bangles, solid cylinder bangles, whether you want to work with metals, plastic, or wood, or whether you want to make plain, embellished or interlocked bangles.

I suggest starting small and simple —like some of the multiple projects provided in the book— and work your way up to more intricate designs.

*You should also invest in several jewelry tools and equipment because the type of project dictates the supplies you will require.

Aside from bangle-making being fun and simple, it also boosts your level of creativity and coordination, and you'll be having a fun time while improving your mundane skills at the same time.

How to Make Bangles

Also remember that it is okay if your first few projects don't turn out perfect; you'll get the hang of it in time as you continue to practice.

With that said, I wish you all the best on your first project!